Clothes in Hot Weather

Miriam Moss

Wayland

Costumes and Clothes

Children's Clothes
Clothes in Cold Weather
Clothes in Hot Weather
Fashionable Clothes
Hair and Make-up
How Clothes Are Made
National Costume
Sports Clothes
Theatrical Costume
Uniforms
Working Clothes

First published in 1988 by Wayland (Publishers) Ltd
61 Western Road, Hove, East Sussex BN3 1JD.

Consultant: Roger Howarth, the multi-cultural adviser for East Sussex
Editor: Deborah Elliott
Designer: Joyce Chester
Cover: Fulani women in Nigeria
wearing beautifully-patterned clothes.

British Library Cataloguing in Publication Data
Moss, Miriam
Clothes in hot weather. — Costumes and clothes).
1. Clothing and dress — Tropical conditions
— Juvenile literature
I. Title   II. Series
646.3 '0913   GT518

ISBN 1-85210-102-4

Photosetting by Direct Image Photosetting, Burgess Hill, West Sussex

Printed in Italy by G. Canale & C.S.p.A., Turin
Bound in France by A.G.M.

Some words in this book are
printed in **bold.** Their meanings
are explained in the glossary on
page 30.

Contents

Hot Weather

There are many different kinds of clothes worn by people all over the world in hot weather. Certain materials and colours are suitable for hot conditions, and it is interesting to see the many ways these have been adapted by different people according to their culture, climate and lifestyle. In this book we shall look at the clothing worn by people who live in permanently hot climates and also by those people who live in countries that have hot weather only at certain times of the year. The examples are not typical of everyone from that country or culture. They illustrate the wide range of clothing worn in hot weather all over the world. The term 'European-style clothing' describes a style of dress common to most countries of the world — suits, jeans and T-shirts are examples of this way of dressing. The term does not refer to clothes worn solely in Europe. Modern or western dress are terms that are also sometimes used.

There are three main types of hot weather: the hot, wet weather found in the tropics, the hot, dry weather found in desert regions and the **temperate** warm summer weather of the middle **latitudes.** The map on pages 8 and 9 shows the areas of the world which

In temperate countries people often wear shorts, T-shirts, sneakers and sun hats on warm, sunny days.

Above In hot weather in China, people often wear wide-brimmed hats to shade their eyes from the sun and loose, cotton clothes.

Below Temperatures in the Caribbean are often high. Notice the variety of cool clothes worn by the women waiting on the jetty.

experience these different types of hot weather. Along the **Equator,** there is a belt of rich, tropical forest. Because the weather here is very hot and wet, people wear light clothing to keep cool in the **humid** atmosphere.

Much of the land which lies along the **tropics of Capricorn and Cancer** is desert, where it seldom rains. The deserts lying north of the Equator include those of the south-western USA and Mexico, the Sahara and the Arabian deserts, and the Thar desert in India. Below the Equator lie the Atacama desert in South America, the Namib in Africa, and the vast deserts of Australia. The weather in these regions is very hot and dry. People who live in the Sahara desert, for example, wear long, loose robes which cover them almost completely. These clothes protect them from

These Tuareg men live in the desert region of Algeria. They wear loose robes and headgear for protection in the dry, dusty conditions.

the burning sun but also allow air to flow over the skin and cool it.

Still further from the Equator lie the lands which have a temperate climate. This is a warm summer and a cool or cold winter. Countries such as New Zealand, Japan, Canada, the Scandinavian countries, Britain and Central and Eastern European countries all experience temperate summers. Some people living in these regions wear cool, cotton clothes in the summer. Often, however, they need to carry another layer of clothing like a jumper, as the weather is changeable.

Above The hot weather in India is sometimes interrupted by heavy monsoon rains. Even when it is wet, however, it is still hot enough to wear cool *saris* and *dhotis*.

Right This young boy in Sydney, Australia is going to school on a skateboard. Because the weather is warm and sunny he is wearing shorts and a cool shirt.

Hot Lands

The map below shows the different areas of the world that experience hot weather.

The dry, dusty sand dunes of the desert in Namibia, South West Africa.

The foothills of Nepal during a monsoon, when the weather is warm and wet.

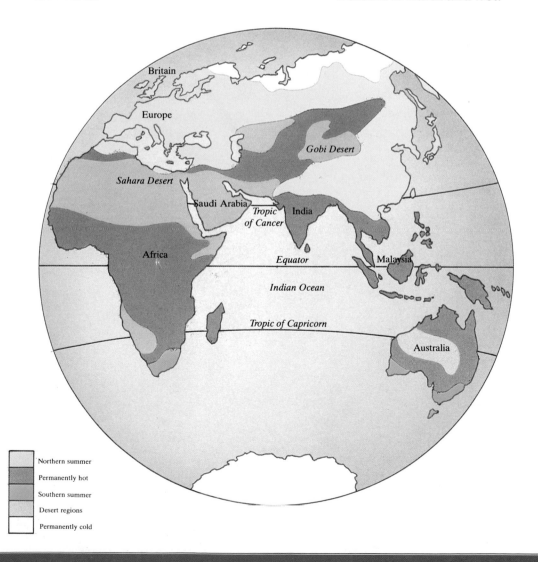

Northern summer
Permanently hot
Southern summer
Desert regions
Permanently cold

Clothes in Hot, Dry Weather

Working clothes

People wear different types of clothes in hot, dry weather, depending on the type of work they do. Much of Brazil, in South America, is dry, flat land where the weather is very hot. In the south are the grasslands where the Brazilian and Argentine **gauchos** work on ranches as cowboys. They wear billowy trousers called **bobbachas** which are full at the waist and narrow at the ankle so that they fit into their knee-length, leather boots.

Their wide, buckled belts have several pockets in which they carry a watch and money. A piece of leather, called a 'chap', is wrapped around the waist and covers one leg. This serves as an apron and also protects the gauchos if cattle rub against them. A **bandana** is worn around the neck and pulled up over the face in a dust storm.

In the very hot and dry parts of India, women work in the towns and in the country wearing *saris*. The *sari* is a draped garment which is very cool and comfortable to wear.

Look at the text and see if you can name the special billowy trousers and bright neck scarf worn by this Argentine *gaucho*. Can you see his leather boots?

Above Can you see the different ways that these Indian women are wearing their beautifully coloured saris?

Below Many offices are air-conditioned. This means people can wear ties and jackets inside when the weather outside is hot.

It has been worn by women all over India for about 2,000 years. It is made of a very long strip of printed material which is often brightly coloured. Women wear their *saris* in a particular way depending on which part of India they come from.

In many parts of the world, people working in towns wear a mixture of traditional and European-style dress. For example, in Cairo, you might see an Egyptian businessman in a pin-striped business suit and a traditional head-dress.

All over the world, people who work in towns and cities wear modern suits. In hot climates offices are often **air-conditioned,** so it is not uncomfortable to work all day wearing a shirt and tie, even if the temperature outside is soaring.

People who work in the open air, however, are exposed to the hot sun all day. They need to wear clothes that keep them cool and comfortable, and allow air to circulate freely.

Many Indian farmers, for example, wear cotton shirts and traditional *dhotis*. A *dhoti* is a length of cotton or silk which is wrapped around the lower half of the body. The different ways in which it is worn varies according to the region. In many parts of Africa, people who work in the countryside wear practical cotton clothes which are ideally suited to the hot weather.

Desert clothes

Deserts form in areas where little rain falls and a baking hot sun dries out the land. Little vegetation can grow in this climate and life can be very hard. Many people work in deserts all over the world. They herd camels, sheep or goats, lay oil pipelines, dig irrigation trenches and drill for oil and other minerals. Often the coolest clothes to wear in the hot, dry conditions are shorts or a cool dress, with a hat to shield the head from the heat of the sun.

Not everyone needs to protect themselves from the sun by wearing a particular kind of clothing. Many people have managed to

Left This cattle hand, working in the dry Australian desert, is wearing a cotton shirt to keep cool.

Below People who work in the desert need cool clothes. These men, who are fixing their truck, are dressed in cotton shorts which absorb the sweat from their bodies.

Left The Tuareg people live in the mountains at the edge of the Sahara desert. Like many people who live and work in the desert they protect themselves from the sun's rays and against the wind by completely covering their bodies.

Below It is traditional for these Algerian women to cover themselves from head to foot. Their cool, white robes reflect the heat.

conquer the harsh conditions in which they live and have adapted to their hot climate. The Bindibu, for example, are a group of Australian **Aborigines** who live comfortably in the vast, flat Australian **outback.** About one third of Australia is desert and it is the smallest and most arid **continent.** The Bindibu do not need to protect themselves against the hot sun by wearing much clothing.

The Tuareg are **nomadic** people who live and work in the mountains on the edge of the Sahara desert. They wear a long length of light cotton, called a **tanguelmoust,** which is arranged in a special way. Their clothes protect them from the fierce heat of the sun and the dry winds. Lighter colours do not absorb heat as much as dark colours. The Tuareg wear white robes which reflect the sun's rays and help to keep their bodies cool.

Bedouin

The Bedouin are desert dwellers who have travelled with their camels, goats and sheep in the deserts of Arabia and North Africa for over 2,000 years. Today, many Bedouin have moved into the towns. Others prefer to stay in the desert, living in the traditional way. In summer, the desert sands shimmer with intense heat. The sun beats down from a cloudless sky and scorching winds frequently blow from the heart of the desert, bringing dust and sandstorms. The temperature at noon can soar to 50°C.

The desert Bedouin dress to suit these harsh conditions. They wear clothes that cover them from head to foot to shield them from the burning sun. Many Bedouin men and women, wear loose, flowing robes which provide good **ventilation.** The wide sleeves allow air to flow over the skin.

Most Bedouin clothes are made of cotton. Cotton is an excellent material for hot weather, because it is **permeable** and lets air flow through it. When the temperature drops sharply at night they wrap wool coverings around themselves for extra warmth.

Some Bedouin men wear _keffiyeh_. These are large cotton kerchiefs kept in place by a double band of black cord. They protect the head from the sun.

Men wear white clothes while women wear many-coloured flowery prints in reds, blues or black and embroidered with coloured threads.

A Bedouin man living in the desert in Libya is likely to wear a long, white, cotton shirt and trousers. On special occasions he wears a coloured waistcoat, and *jerd* — a long piece of woollen material — which he drapes around his body, pulling it over his head when he needs extra protection. Women wear long, cotton dresses with a woollen band tied around their waists. Over their heads they wear black, cotton scarves. Many Bedouin in Saudi Arabia wear an outer garment called an *abba*. This is a long black or brown sleeveless, woollen coat, without fastenings.

Left **This Bedouin family are wearing a mixture of traditional and European-type clothing.**

Can you see how the Bedouin girls pictured below have protected their heads from the sun?

Chapter 4

Clothes in Hot, Wet Weather

Indians of the Amazon

In the Amazon basin in South America there are large areas of tropical rainforest that are rich in vegetation. Huge trees with enormous roots and tangled lianas (climbing plants) are home to an assortment of wild animals and insects. The weather is hot, wet and humid and there are frequent rainstorms. The Amazonian Indians live here. They are nomadic hunters who move from place to place in search of food.

The Amazonian Indians have adapted to their climate by making full use of their surroundings. For example, the Yaqua Indians, from the Amazon region of Peru, wear skirts made from grasses which are cool and extremely comfortable.

These girls, walking to school in a tropical storm in the Amazon, wear light uniforms and carry umbrellas.

In parts of the Amazon basin, where the weather is hot and humid, people find it comfortable to wear light clothing.

They are expert weavers and weave cotton on looms into hammocks, slings and waistbands. In some communities they weave **cushmas**, which are long, poncho-like garments. The Uracare Indians make cloth from the bark of trees.

Some groups of Indians have given up their traditional dress completely and now wear European-style clothing. Other groups, like the Shipibo, have partly retained their traditional dress. Many women wear traditional skirts of hand-woven cotton, with blouses. The men usually wear jeans and shirts but often wear *cushmas* for special occasions.

Southeast Asia and the Pacific

In the Pacific islands such as Tonga, Fiji and Western Samoa, the weather is always hot and wet. Men and women alike wear the *sarong* (a long piece of cloth tucked around the waist or armpits) or European-style dress. Traditional dress is often worn for special occasions. Tongans sometimes wear fine mats wrapped around their bodies to weddings, and Tahitians dress up in long, grass skirts and head-dresses to dance. Dancing clothes vary throughout the Pacific Islands but the clothes are usually made of leaves, flowers, feathers and grass.

Many Malaysians wear European-style dress. Some Malay women wear a *sarung,* a loose, ankle-length skirt, with a *kebaya,* which is a blouse fastened at the front. Malaysia is famous for its *kain songet.* This is a cloth embroidered with gold thread which comes in one colour like blue, maroon, purple, green or yellow. Men and women often wear this cloth at ceremonial functions, especially at weddings. Clothes made of batik, a patterned, dyed cloth, are also worn.

In southern China, where the weather can often be very hot and humid, many men and women wear the same kind of clothing. They wear loose cotton trousers and long jackets or **singlets** which, until recently, were in various shades of blue or olive green. Today, many Chinese people buy stylish clothes.

The couple being escorted to their wedding in Malaysia are wearing clothes made from *kain songet*. This is a material embroidered with gold thread.

Cotton clothes are worn for everyday use but the clothes worn for special occasions are often made of silk. These clothes are woven in lovely designs and bright colours. Brocades, velvets, and silk and nylon mixtures are used. Silk trouser suits embroidered with dragons or flowers in gold thread are sometimes worn. Special regional costumes include flowing skirts, striped aprons and colourful and amazing head-dresses.

Right Loose, white, cotton clothes are the most suitable in hot weather. This girl from the Pacific Islands wears a cool dress.

Below Look at the brightly-coloured clothes worn by these Chinese children. They are wearing cool, cotton tops and patterned trousers.

Africa

There are a vast assortment of clothes worn in the different African countries. These are influenced by whether people work in towns or in the countryside and by the climate. The materials and colours are carefully chosen to meet the demands of the weather. The coast of Kenya in East Africa has a hot, wet climate. In the coastal towns many women and men wear T-shirts, shorts and jeans. Kenyan women who work on the *shambas* (farms) in the countryside often dress in beautiful, bright colours. They wear a mixture of styles. Some wear dresses in cotton materials with a colourful scarf on their heads to protect them from the hot sun. Others wear *kangas*. These are brightly coloured pieces of cotton, often patterned with Kenyan **proverbs** written on them. They are very cool and are worn wrapped around the body, or as a skirt, wrapped around the waist.

Above Business people all over the world wear similar clothes, despite the climate. These men are from Kenya.

Left Hausa girls wearing clothes made from highly-coloured material.

Red is the traditional mourning colour of the Ashanti people. Notice the variety of patterns and styles worn by these women.

In West Africa, where it is very hot and humid, many Africans live and work in towns. They wear suits and ties or dresses to work in the offices and industries. After work they often change into traditional clothes made of cool cotton. Outside the towns some people wear traditional African clothes which are made of brightly printed fabrics, arranged in many different styles but always without zips or buttons. Head-dresses are usually made from matching materials. The Yoruba wear colourful gowns, called *agbada,* which are often striped. These are made of cotton using modern prints and dyes. The **Hausa** also wear gowns and head-dresses, but in white. Important Hausa wear gowns of a single colour which are finely stitched and embroidered in symbolic patterns.

Important Hausa men from Nigeria wear loose gowns richly embroidered with symbolic patterns. Many also wear head protection.

Chapter 5

Temperate Climates

In temperate climates, summers are usually warm, and sometimes temperatures can be quite high. The clothes worn in hot weather are made from materials designed to keep the wearer cool and comfortable. Skirts come in many shapes and styles, from wrap around knee-length ones made of cheesecloth, to miniskirts made of leather. They are zipped, buttoned and tied, pleated or flared. Sun dresses come in many different colours made out of cool materials such as cotton or linen.

Casual tops are equally varied. Teenagers all over the world wear T-shirts and vests, often with bright slogans written on them, in hot weather. Long- and short-sleeved blouses and

In hot weather, the least amount of clothes are required when playing sport, as exercise can make you even hotter.

Above **These children playing in the shade during their school summer holidays are wearing shorts and T-shirts.**

shirts are worn with cotton cardigans and sweat shirts, which come in a multitude of colours and styles. Lightweight tracksuits in pastel shades are popular, as are zipper jackets made of cotton, nylon or synthetic mixes.

Trouser styles vary from loose, baggy, cotton trousers with turned-up hems to skin-tight jeans made of striped or stone-washed denim. Shorts are held up with belts, drawstrings or elastic and are fastened with buckles, buttons, poppers or hooks. Tailored jackets and trousers or jackets and skirts, made from cotton, linen or leather, are worn for more formal occasions.

Right **A selection of brightly-coloured cotton clothes and sun hats from a shop in Marbella, Spain.**

Beach Clothes

Beach clothes are worn in hot weather all over the world. Europeans flock to the Mediterranean coast in the summer. Some Africans go to coastal resorts such as Mombasa, which are also popular with tourists from all over the world. The beautiful Australian beaches are popular places as are the West Indian and Pacific Islands. South and Central Americans enjoy the warm sea and sands of the Mexican and Brazilian coastlines. Many people are lucky enough to live and work by lakes or by the sea in hot weather. For them, beach clothes are not holiday clothes but a part of everyday life. These lightweight clothes keep them cool during the day.

On beaches all over the world, people wear T-shirts, shorts and swimming costumes. It is interesting to see the many different colours and fashions. Bermuda shorts and colourful vests are popular everywhere. Male beachwear can vary from large boxer shorts with palm trees printed on them to extremely brief swimming trunks. They are usually made

Melanesian women playing cricket on the beach. Notice their cool, batik dresses which are in their team colours.

of cool cotton, or stretchy viscose and polyester mixtures. Female beachwear comes in all shapes and sizes. There are bikinis with shoulder straps, **halter necks** or no straps at all. Swimming costumes are plain or patterned and in any colour from black to orange or pink. They cover a variety of styles from cutaway legs to the fuller-skirted variety. Most are made from synthetic fibres, but some are made of flannel, crochet cotton or even lace.

People often like to wrap strips of brightly-printed cotton material around their body. This fashion has always been popular with women in Africa and the Pacific Islands, and is extremely practical in hot weather.

Above Lifeguards have to wear clothes which can be easily spotted by other people. They also need clothes that keep them cool on the hot beach.

Left How many different kinds of swimsuits can you see in this picture of the Copacabana beach in Brazil?

Chapter 7

Headgear and Footwear

Headgear

Hats are a very important form of protection against heatstroke which can make people very ill. Heatstroke occurs when your head and body are unprotected by clothes or a hat and the hot sun beats down for long periods.

Sun hats come in all sorts of shapes, sizes and materials. There are the peaked, canvas baseball caps, the perspex, peaked sunhats without a crown called visors, the **panama** and the South American gaucho's wide-brimmed hat.

Headgear also protects people when the dry wind whips up the sand during a sandstorm. Then desert travellers pull their head

A selection of hats.

coverings right over their faces. This protects their eyes and stops the sand from filling their nostrils and mouths and choking them. Some Arabian Bedouin wear camel-hair caps with a kerchief on top called a *keffiyeh*. This is held in place by a double band of black cord. Some Libyan Bedouin wear white **skullcaps** with perhaps a strip of cotton wound round to make a turban.

Headgear is also connected with tradition and religion. Sikh women wear *dupattas* (scarves) to cover their heads during services at *gurdwaras* (Sikh temples). Sikh men keep their hair covered with turbans. In Egypt, some men wear the traditional fez, and in Malaysia some boys wear a *mini telekong*. Zulu women of South Africa often wear broad, saucer-shaped hats to show they are married.

Chinese men and women wear small, peaked hats to shade their eyes from the sun. Many Chinese farmers wear a wide-brimmed bamboo sun hat, called a *hakka*. Some Yoruba girls from Nigeria wear brightly coloured turbans called *asoi-oke*. These are skilfully held in place by wrapping and folding them around the head.

These Japanese schoolchildren are wearing peaked, red and green sun hats to shade their eyes and heads from the bright sun.

Footwear

Shoes are worn to protect the feet. They need to be cool and a comfortable fit especially in hot weather. Footwear in hot weather comes in all shapes, sizes and materials. There are leather sandals which are flat, high-heeled, low-heeled or slingback. The leather can be lattice-worked, plain or with patterned holes punched through it. This allows the air to circulate and cool the foot but also gives protection to the wearer.

Children often wear moulded plastic beach sandals in bright colours. They are especially useful for swimming or walking over wet, uncomfortable surfaces. They protect the feet without making them too hot and uncomfortable. Sports shoes, like plimsolls and trainers, are often worn for everyday use in hot weather because they are designed to be comfortable and cool to wear.

In very hot, dry conditions some people wear desert boots, sometimes called safari boots, which are made of suede. They are light, comfortable and allow the feet to 'breathe' (let air in and out). Their rubber soles protect feet from the burning sand and rocks of dry scrubland. Flip-flops, which are cool to wear, are worn worldwide. They are made entirely of plastic and are therefore cheap to manufacture. However, they are not very long-lasting and do not give very much protection to the feet.

Some traditional footwear, like clogs originally from Holland, and Chinese black pumps, have become fashionable in other

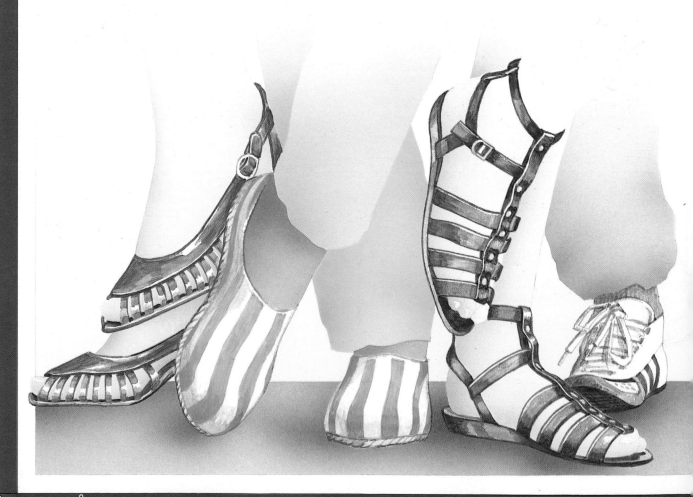

parts of the world. Espadrilles, that originally came from France, are now worn in many countries. They are light and comfortable and so are very suitable for hot weather. They have canvas uppers and rope soles and come in bright, plain colours or stripes, with wedge or flat heels.

Right The woman in the picture is wearing a pair of plastic flip-flops. The girl on the right is wearing plastic sandals.

Below Illustrations of hot weather footwear. From left to right: peep-toe sling-backs, espadrilles, leather sandals, trainers, flip-flops, jellies, canvas pumps.

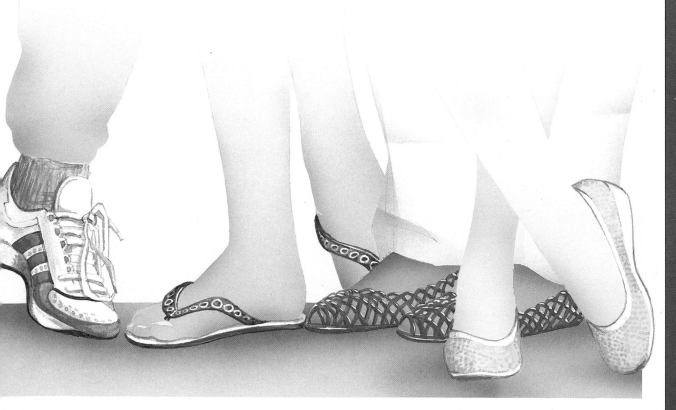

Glossary

Aborigines   The original inhabitants of a country. Today, the term specifically refers to the original inhabitants of Australia.

Air-conditioned   Offices or buildings that are air-conditioned have a temperature that is kept at a steady level.

Bandana   A brightly coloured kerchief worn around the neck.

Continent   The world's land surface is divided into five continents: Africa, North and South America, Asia, Australia and Europe.

Equator   An imaginary line making a circle around the earth, halfway between the North and South Poles.

Evaporate   To change from a liquid to a vapour — mist or steam — or to fade away altogether.

Gauchos   Cowboys from South America.

Halter necks   Tops which are fastened behind the neck and waist, leaving the back and arms bare.

Hausa   A group of people of West Africa, living mainly in northern Nigeria.

Heatstroke   A feverish illness which occurs if someone stays out too long in very hot weather.

Humid   A moist, damp atmosphere.

Latitudes   The distance of a place north or south of the Equator. It is measured in degrees. 1° is about 110km.

Nomadic   People who wander with their animals from place to place.

Outback   The remote bush country of Australia.

Panama   A hat made of plaited leaves of the jipijapa plant of Central and South America.

Permeable   A material which heat or air can easily pass through.

Proverbs   Well-known and wise sayings which usually have a moral.

Singlets   Sleeveless vests that are usually worn with shorts.

Skullcap   A rounded cap without a brim which fits the crown of the head.

Temperate   Weather that is moderate and not extreme. The temperate areas of the world lie between the tropics and the polar regions.

Tropics of Capricorn and Cancer   The tropic of Capricorn is the line of latitude at about 23½° south of the Equator; the tropic of Cancer is the line of latitude at about 23½° north of the Equator.

Ventilation   Clothes that have ventilation are loose enough to allow air to move freely around the body and so keep it cool.

Books to read

Bedouin — The Nomads of the Desert by Muhammad Alotaibi (Wayland [Publishers] Ltd, 1986)

China, the Land and its Peoples by Anna Merton and Shio-yun Kan (Macdonald Educational, 1974)

Costumes and Clothes by Jean Cooke (Wayland [Publishers] Ltd, 1986)

Geography — Landscapes, Climates and People by Dougal Dixon (Franklin Watts, 1983)

Indians of the Amazon by Marion Morrison (Wayland [Publishers] Ltd, 1985)

Just Look at Clothes by Brenda Ralph Lewis (Macdonald Educational, 1985)

Looking at Iran by Janine Weidel (A & C Black Publishers Ltd, 1978)

Looking at Lands, Australia by Robert Moore (Macdonald Educational, 1983)

South Pacific Islanders by Vilsoni & Patricia Hereniko (Wayland [Publishers] Ltd, 1985)

Summer by Ralph Whitlock (Wayland [Publishers] Ltd, 1986)

Living Here Series (Wayland [Publishers] Ltd, 1986)

Index

Acknowledgements

The Publisher would like to thank the following for providing the pictures used in this book: Bruce Coleman Ltd 9 (top), 11 (top), 13 (top), 19 (bottom); Format Photographers 11 (bottom), 20 (top); The Hutchison Library 12 (both), 21 (top), 23 (bottom); Preben Kristensen 15 (top); Marion and Tony Morrison 16, 17, 25 (left); Christine Osborne 14, 23 (bottom); Topham Picture Library 12 (top), 25; Malcolm S. Walker 8-9, 26, 28-9; Wayland Picture Library 5 (both), 7 (bottom), 10, 18, 25 (top); John Wright 4, 22 (bottom); ZEFA 5 (top), 6, 7, (top), 13 (bottom), 15 (bottom), 19 (top), 20 (bottom), 21 (bottom), 23 (top), 27 (bottom).